THE WINDMILLS OF THE MIND

A Collection of Poems of Love and Regret

WENDELL WILLKIE NEWMAN

WAKEFIRE
PRESS

The Windmills of the Mind: A Collection of Poems of Love and Regret

Copyright © 2022 Wendell Willkie Newman

Cover Design by Dee Dee Book Covers
Illustrations by Gail Starck

ISBN:
978-1-950476-37-4 (Paperback)
978-1-950476-36-7 (eBook)

Published by:

WAKEFIRE
PRESS

CONTENTS

A Note from the Author   vii

If   1
The Flight of the Golden Butterfly   2
IM a Butterfly   3
Written in the Stars   5
Drowning in the Sea of Love   6
A Whisper in the Night   8
The Foolish Young Man   9
I Would Love to Be   10
The Lady and the Tiger   13
Mind Speak   15
The Perfect Design   16
An Early Morning Walk   17
Windmills of the Mind   19
The Old Man and the Butterfly   20
The Old Poet   21
Too Old   22
Just the Backward Walking Man   23
The Weeping Poet   25
A Cold Night in Edinburgh   26
A Hole in the Heart   28
Betrayed   29
Branded   30
Burning Bridges   31
Hanging by a Thread   33
Don't Let the Bed Bugs Bite   34
Fancy   36
Filled   37
How Many Tears Must I Cry?   38

The Fading of the Tears 39

Tick Tock 41

Had My Heart 42

I Am String 43

I Wanna Be Me Again 44

Once in a Lifetime 46

You Are 47

His Melody 49

Longing for Your Beauty 50

Illusions 51

Reflections 52

Footprints 53

The Goldie Oldie Man 54

Love Letters of the Mind 55

Angel Wings 56

You Bless My Day 57

Seasons 58

Bonding of the Soul 59

You Are That 60

For the Sound of Your Voice 61

A Case of Missing You 63

Cottage by the Sea 65

The Last Goodbye 66

The Journey 67

Acknowledgments 71

To the Dreamers and Romantics not bound by age

Inside I write to you with simplicity so that you may feel my words as they touch you: heart, mind and soul.

A NOTE FROM THE AUTHOR

I would love to share with you some of the events which inspired my poems.

Regret:

The year was 1958. We were pen pals. Three years later she was sweet sixteen. I was 19. I traveled 300 miles to meet her. I felt love at first sight.

I promised to return but mountains got in my way and she was lost to me, forever. Twenty-five years later, I found her. She was as unhappy as I.

I began to write the regret poems. Some of the words are embellished but the heartache, tears, pain, and misery are real. In fact, memories still blow into the windmills some sixty years later. I still cry each time I read. My regret still hurts. God oh God please stop the windmills from turning.

The golden butterfly and poems of love:

Some forty years after losing sweet little sixteen, using the World Wide Web, I found an international pen pal in the Republic of Ireland, some 3000 miles away.

She was in her forties with big blue eyes, golden hair and a lovely face. She became the golden butterfly. Both *The Flight of the Golden Butterfly* and *IM a Butterfly* were inspired by instant message sessions.

When I read her first mail, I discovered a mind which was so brilliant, it sparkled with inspiration for my poetic mind.

We became best of friends. I found her words so inspiring. I wrote and sent her many poems. I told her she was my inspiration, and she replied with the following:

You don't need any inspiration Wendell, when you have poetry inside you and that God-given gift. It will find a way out no matter what. It is a beautiful poem and I love it but then, everything you have written has made me feel wonderful or thoughtful or laugh or cry. It's always touched me in so many ways and that Wendell is down to that gift you have, and as we are talking of poetry you should be sorted out now. Isn't that so?

Jan.

Jan loved my poems. Hopefully you will too.

Enjoy my book,
Wendell

IF

If I were to have my way
And this is so very true
I would spend my lifetime
Just sitting and thinking of you
For when I think
Of your golden hair
My life spins by
Without a worry or a care
Finding in my daydreams
That my future lies
Far into the depths
Of your lovely blue eyes
And just to think of all
The love which could unfold
From within the depths
Of your golden immortal soul
I find you so beautiful
Completely through and through
I could spend the rest of my life
Just sitting and thinking of you

THE FLIGHT OF THE GOLDEN BUTTERFLY

Come, go with me
Said the Golden Butterfly to I
Let us just not see…
How high we can fly
Wing to wing she led him
Into the night sky of crystal blue
The butterfly named I
And the golden butterfly named… you
Infinite are the boundaries
Of just how high one can transcend
When you are the butterfly named I
And have a Golden Butterfly friend
She took him spiraling, upward and outward
Onward, toward the break of day
Absolutely… utterly… totally
Taking his breath away
Time was and time is, an essence
All sprinkled between the hours
Tasting, oh how sweet is the nectar
While lingering amongst the flowers
Forever, ebbing and flowing are memories
Of this flight so high
That, of the Golden Butterfly
And the butterfly, named I

IM A BUTTERFLY

She said unto him
Come, fly with me today
I will completely
Take your breath away

She led him into
The passage of her mind
Up the spiraling golden stairways
Only the chosen few can climb

She revealed to him such beauty
More than he could behold
As she guided him into
The depths of her soul

He fills up completely
With total emotional bliss
Life is so Magnificent
In a day like this…

He now sleeps so peacefully
Through the lengths of the night
His dream machine replaying the scenes
Of the butterflies in flight

WRITTEN IN THE STARS

Suddenly, here is you and I
The very best of friends
It does really make you wonder
How and why our friendship begins
Could we be by random chance?
Or by intelligent design
Or simply as grains of sand
Blown together, by the winds of time
Shall we forever subsist?
As grains of sand in the wind
As chaotic changes of time
Blow us apart forever, again
Could it be our names?
Are written together in the stars
With a history of all that's past
And a future, which is ours
Surely we are two souls
Etched in the stones of the galaxy
Bonded together forever
Into the future, meant to be
Always cherishing this moment
Of destiny, yours and mine
As we are, forever
Until the end of time

DROWNING IN THE SEA OF LOVE

He gazed upon the sea of love
Waters warmed as by the fire
He felt the compelling drawing
Of its' mystic Ire

Love's waters were so kind
So lovely, love's seashore
He decided to venture in his toe
Perhaps its warmth to adore

How delightful the feeling
Of the gentle ebb tide sublime
Perhaps he could bask in love's warmth
For just a moment in time

His heart is pounding wildly
Drawn from shore by the tidal sweep
Now plunged completely into the sea of love…
Love's raging swirling waters, intensely, deep

Frantic now, he backstrokes
To return once again to shore
As each stroke takes him deeper
Into love's waters than before

Can he now be rescued?
From love's drowning lot
Well, perhaps
Then again, perhaps, not

A WHISPER IN THE NIGHT

He looks into the night
It is half past two
He whispers into the night
I love you.
He whispers into the night
You are a day dream
The loveliest lady
I have ever seen
He whispers to her
The object of his affection
You are absolutely completely
And totally, perfect and perfection
As he whispers into the night
Saying "I love you"
He sometimes wonders
Does she ever whisper, too?

THE FOOLISH YOUNG MAN

Once a prize of great value
Given to a foolish young man
Who held her love carelessly?
In the palm of his hand
Alas, he did not know
That which was given to hold
Was far more precious
Than diamonds, silver or gold
So instead of caressingly
Holding it inside his heart
He opened his hand
As his world came apart
Should he not have realized?
When he opened his hand
His love of a lifetime
Fell to another man
The remainder of his life, agony
As he kept crying night and day
Cause he didn't cherish her love
Until he let it slip away

I WOULD LOVE TO BE

I would love to be
Swept away by the tide
Just to be
By your side

I would love to be
Your kite on a string
Or your dog
On a chain

Would love to be
The floor beneath your feet
Walk on me
Would be so sweet

Would love to be
Putty in your hand
As you mold me
Into the perfect man

Would love to be
A rose or two
So I would be
A fragrance for you

Would love to be
Thoughts from time to time
So you would hold me
In your mind

THE LADY AND THE TIGER

She, the Perfect Lady
Dignity and pride
But lurking is a tiger
Deep, deep, inside

She, the Domesticated Lady
Happy as can be
Inside, the Bengal Tiger
Longing to be free

A Lady of Meekness
There is no doubt
Inside, The tiger, raging
Longing to roar out

A Quandary of contradiction
How can this be?
She remains, always, the Perfect Lady
The tiger remains, always, determined to be free.

gstarck

MIND SPEAK

A whirling grinding motion
Deep inside his head
Whether walking or talking
Or deep asleep in his bed
His mind writes love letters
Without need to stop and think
As his heart mind and emotions
Are completely in total sync
How he adores her beauty
And from time to time
Says she is the most magnificent lady
One could ever find
His longing to touch her soul
In the depth of a kiss
And heaven hasn't felt
A feeling such as this
Spin, spin, spin
Oh how his mind does spin
His mind deletes the letter
Then writes it all over, again

THE PERFECT DESIGN

She is a lovely angel
Made with a heavenly designee
He is an old man
Wrinkled and withered
With the passage of time
He longs for a hug
One which will never quit
For now he and the angel
Are a perfect fit

AN EARLY MORNING WALK

Three in the morning
How wonderful to find
Your footprints, lingering, as
You have just entered into my mind
How wonderful the feeling
As our hearts now beating as one
Hand in hand we walk love's pathway
Our journey has just begun
The flowers along the pathway
Beauty, which I love and adore
How compelling, is the feeling
Of never passing this way before
In the destined moment
Midst the fragrance of lush
Walking through love's doorway
Hearts overflowing with the adrenal rush.

WINDMILLS OF THE MIND

Memories so quickly flowing
Blown by the winds of time
Bring a whirling force of circumstances
Turning the windmills of his mind

It is the twisting of emotions
As the whirling grind
The moments of yesterday
Are blowing in his mind

Comes the wind of precious moments
Tenderness so sweet
Thoughts of the warm kisses
Makes him feel complete

Here blow the heartaches
The sorrow and the pain
As a whirlwind, round and round
Again, again and again

Longing, for the soft warm breeze of happiness
Leave the heartaches all behind
He then can bask in his love for her forever
As the windmills turn gently in his mind.

THE OLD MAN AND THE BUTTERFLY

Weary old man?
Heavy was his load
Struggling along to find
The end of life's road

Tired, worn and anguished
He sits for a spell to linger
As a beautiful young lady butterfly
Lit upon his little finger

Was it his imagination?
Or did she speak his name?
But from this moment on
His life was never the same

The old man still struggles along
Searching for the end of life's road
But oh how much lighter?
Is the weight of his load

THE OLD POET

Was something inside him?
Far beyond his control
As poetic bits of wisdom
Kept flowing from his soul
In moments of inspiration
His truth could be found
He so quickly to hasten
To write his words all down
So precious were his words
He so longed to share
Others did not understand him
Perhaps they did not care.

How he longed to be famous
How he longed to be read
So true, a poet is not famous
Till long after he is dead.

TOO OLD

I long to see
Heaven's door
I'm just too old
To travel anymore

I long to kiss
Lips sweet as wine
I'm just too old
To shake the vine

I reach to touch
A lovely face
They quickly move
It's such a waste

I long for a hug
But I don't dare
All I can do
Is sit here and stare?

It seems with the ladies
I no longer get anywhere
So I'll just keep sitting
In my rocking chair

JUST THE BACKWARD WALKING MAN

Was the backward walking man
For many, many years
Trying to keep from drowning
In his very, own tears

He can see no future
Anywhere ahead
Keeps looking behind him
Wishing he were dead

He saw his future
As it faded away
Just keeps walking backward
Searching for yesterday

If he keeps walking backward
If he goes very, very fast
Perhaps, he can return
To his happy past

THE WEEPING POET

Sat once, the poet weeping
As he repented of his sins
Remembering his broken promises
I shall return again
Repenting in his leisure
Of his sin in haste
Unkept promises, broken dreams
His lifetime of waste
Feeling the glow of love
His mind sees her face again
But for each grain of love
Feels tons and tons of pain
He carefully pens his words
Weeps on every one
His page, wet and soggy
Before the work is done
So many times he reads them
As his tears well up and drop
It seems, he has cried forever
Guess he will never stop

A COLD NIGHT IN EDINBURGH

Was my last holiday night in Edinburgh
I was struggling with the cold
My body frozen beyond belief
All the way to my soul

A bit of mystic in the air
Snowflakes gently falling down
I watched how gracefully
They softly landed to the ground

Was then I brushed the snowflakes
From my closing eyes
I opened them suddenly
What an intriguing surprise

There, the lady of my dreams
Stood poised and picturesque
My mind drank her beauty
My heart pounding wildly in my chest

Golden locks flowed from beneath her hat
As she shivered in the cold
Our eyes connected instantly
Fires of love burning in my soul

We talked, we laughed, we danced

Until the light of dawn
The heartbreaking moment
I must move on

I gave her my heart
We said our last goodbyes
I boarded my plane
Brushed the frozen tear
From my weeping eyes

A HOLE IN THE HEART

Empty heart
Empty mind
No love
Could he find?
For all his life
His heart in doubt
As love flowed in
And Love flows out
One day he discovered
While searching his soul
His heart seemed to have
A large gaping hole
He searched the world
For his solution and then
He found you
And you fit right in
A special gift
From God above
Now his heart is filled
Completely with love
God surely knows
Exactly what to do
As the hole in the heart
Was the exact same size as you?

BETRAYED

I wish my heart
Were as a stone
Then I should not cry
And feel so all alone

It was only
Just the other day
My heart the renegade
Gave himself away

He loves her with all himself
So as you might guess
I have no control
Life is quite a mess

If I would have had a warning
If only I had known
I would have conquered him
And turned him into hard cold stone

BRANDED

He belongs to her, completely
From the very start
As he feels her hot branding iron of love
Searing her name across his heart
Her brand is compelling
Flashing, night and day
Declaring he belongs to her
Keeping all others away
How wonderful is the feeling
Of her name flashing inside his chest
Every heart beat throbbing
You're the best you're the best
How he loves the belonging
As he listens to love's voice
The knowing, everyone else
Is simply, second choice

BURNING BRIDGES

Once, far away at Salt Lick
Flowed a river of salty tears
Was a bridge built of her memories?
Spanning all his passing years
His soul is flooded with pain, misery and
    heartaches
Each time he comes to cross
His eyes flowing in constant sorrow
Heart mind and soul suffering the loss
If only he had burning bridges
Left them all behind
He wouldn't ever cross them again
And find peace in his mind
But he cannot remove her precious memory
So as to take away his pain
He cannot burn the bridges
Monuments immortalizing her name
He just keeps crossing the bridges
Through all his fleeting years
Perhaps one day his sorrow will flow away
Into the river of his tears

HANGING BY A THREAD

Was a time
I was hanging by a thread
Twisting in the wind
Fearing I were dead
You came to me
As an angel in white
Lit my world
With a golden light
Now you say
You are hanging by a thread
Twisting in the wind
Fearing you were dead
So, I pray, God
Send her an angel in white
Light up her world
With a golden light
Now how happy are we
For all the world to see
Walking on the thread,
You and me

DON'T LET THE BED BUGS BITE

I was fast asleep
In my bed
Butterflies flying
Inside my head
When I was awakened
In the mid of night
By this huge bug
What a dreadful sight
I cried out
How can this be?
A bed bug
Large as me
She was in that way
I could tell
From the intense manner
Of her screams and yell
She says, to me,
You shall be alright
But I must give you
Just one little bite
Now little bugs, crawling
All over the place
I see my image
In their lovely little face
The best explanation
I can clearly say

Must have absorbed
Some of my DNA
So now I
Completely understand
The ageless wisdom
Given down to man
It does not matter
How fierce the fight
"DON'T LET THE BED BUGS BITE"

FANCY

Fancy is
I would be inclined
For a bit of candy
From time to time
Fancy is
My face turning red
From the fantasies
Playing inside my head
Fancy is
Dreams passing by
Building sand castles
Way up high in the sky
Fancy is
When someone passes me by
I say to myself
My, oh my, oh my,
Fancy to me is
A word meaning love
And how I hope
And dream of
So if the last verse
Is surely true
Oh how
I fancy you

FILLED

You have filled my heart
You have filled my soul
With more love
Than I can possibly hold
I long to enter the portals
Of your soul
Fill you with more love
Than you can possibly hold
Now completely filled with love
Heart, soul and mind
We can bask in our love, forever
Until the end of time

HOW MANY TEARS MUST I CRY?

As often as I think of you
As my mind calls out your name
My heart begins pounding
Temperature to a raging burning flame

And as I think of you
Through all my passing years
The sorrow in my heart
Brings a flood of hot salty and bitter tears

As the bitter tears
Come large, hot and fast I cry
GOD OH MY GOD
How long will this last

I'll cry all of my tomorrows
I cry now and yesterday
GOD OH GOD
Will this pain never pass away?

As I cry tomorrow today and my yesterday
Knowing, you are the reason why
Will this hurt never never end
How many tears must I cry?

THE FADING OF THE TEARS

All of my salty tears
Forever flowing across my face
Removing the black from my beard
Leaving grey in its place
All the pain in my mind
Is removing the brown from my hair
Now all winter grey
As it is just lingering there
All the tears through the years
Keep falling from my eyes
Removing the baby blue
From my sunny skies
And all these salty lonesome tears
I keep crying time after time
Is leaving these tired ole eyes
Colorless, glazed and color blind

TICK TOCK

Sitting in my cottage
Is my ole grandfather's clock
It just sits there ticking
Tick tock tick tock

For this lonely old man
I hear this clock calling your name
And my mind sees your face
Again again again and again

Tick tock tick tock tick tock
As my heart beats with this clock
Will this tick tock tick tock
Never never, ever never stop

Tick tock tick tock
As my heart strings pull down the tears
Tick is for heart ache tock is for the tears
Tick tock tick tocking for years, years and years

This old clock has
Its own mind and spring of stainless steel
I pray it will stop tick tocking
But I guess it never will

HAD MY HEART

Were my heart
A mortal place
I could be
Your resting place
Had my heart
A roof and door
You could live there
Forevermore
Were my heart furnished
And complete
You could sit a spell
Rest your feet
Well my heart
Has all the above
And tons and tons
And tons of love
If my heart had arms
Which could reach your soul?
It is you
I could forever hold.

I AM STRING

I am string
Wrap me around your finger
My love for you
Shall forever linger
Roll me into a ball
Really really tight
Play with me
I'll never struggle or fight
I am strong
And flexible you know
You may turn me into
Your yo-yo
I am string
Wrap me around your finger
You are will
I am surrender

I WANNA BE ME AGAIN

I wanna be me again
Were the words she said?
As clouds of gloom and doom
Were billowing inside her head

So divine the inspiration
Of knowing what to do
She will rebuild herself
And be good as new

So great was this moment
Of knowing where to start
As she quickly disassembled
All the portions of her heart

Gingerly dusting them
With faith, hope and charity
Soon found them
New as could be

She was so amazed
With her surprising find
Brushing away the cobwebs of discouragement
Which were lurking inside her mind

She then dusted the reaches

Of her immortal soul
Soon was shining
Brightly as polished gold

She then assembled
All of her back together
She was now me again
And seven times better

ONCE IN A LIFETIME

Looking into your eyes
Kissing the beauty of your lips
Breathing your breath
Holding your face in my fingertips
Basking in your ambiance
Hour by hour by hour
Feeling the grasping
Of being in love's power
The beating of hearts
As they record the time
Of perfect memories
Of love and joy, sublime
The destined feeling of belonging
Of Your soul and mine
Love in perfection
You are, my once in a lifetime.

YOU ARE

You are my life
You are my hope
You are my anchor
My lifeline rope
You are the thoughts
Which I always find
Entering the portals
Of my mind
You are my longing
My heart's desire
You are the source
Which lights my fire?
You are the spirit
Inside of me
You are forever
For eternity

HIS MELODY

Once in a lifetime
Someone comes along
To give him the melody
To the words of life's song
Sweetly she plays inside his heart
He wonders how this can be
The sweetest music on earth
Heaven's great symphony
Her melody is the sweetest
His heart has ever heard
It says absolutely everything
And he no longer needs his words

LONGING FOR YOUR BEAUTY

Longing, for your beauty
For my hunger to taste
Seeing, the work of art
Etched, in your face
It is the eternal longing
For your beauty to behold
You are the wind in my sails
The fire in my soul
You are the red
In the mellow wine
As you spin my heart
You dazzle my mind
It is the thoughts
Of your beauty to behold
Fulfills the longing of a lifetime
Fills my heart, mind and soul

ILLUSIONS

Is it possible?
Reality, is not as it seems
Perhaps, I have just imagined you
Perhaps you are only a dream
Is it possible?
You do not have wings of white
As our thoughts communicate
In the middle of the night
Could it be?
I imagined you lifted me higher
Filled my heart full of love
Setting my soul on fire
If you are just an illusion
Oh so very quickly
I must say
I love you dearly
Before my illusion fades away

REFLECTIONS

If only you could see
Into his heart's mirror's glow
There to see your beauty
From your head to your toe
Should you but see yourself?
Through the writer's eyes
You would find yourself to be
Beautiful, witty, wonderful and wise
Were you in a galaxy?
Away in the sky oh so far
Everyone would see you
As God's brightest star

FOOTPRINTS

I feel your footprint
Time after time
As I feel you gently
Walking in my mind

Oh how I love to feel
The prints of your feet
So wonderfully beautiful
Delicate and eloquently sweet

I feel you tiptoe
Into the warmth of my heart
Bringing so much sweetness
Which shall never depart?

You give so much happiness
My mind does overflow
As I feel your footprints
Dancing, in my soul

I feel so loved
As time after time
I can feel your footprints
As you are walking in my mind

THE GOLDIE OLDIE MAN

Now just an old man
Feeling sad and low
Listening to his heart ache
On the Goldie Oldie show

Searching for the happiness
Of his careless past
Wondering.... where did love go
Why, did it not last?

Calling to request their old song
Time after time
Refreshing the memories
Of happiness in his mind

Says he, play *The Lion Sleeps Tonight*
Each time he calls in
He replays the happiness
Remembering who, where and when

Searching for his youth
As he has now grown old
Just sitting and listening
To the Goldie Oldie show

LOVE LETTERS OF THE MIND

I begin to write
Time after time
The phrases of my feelings
As a love letter in my mind
As my words serenade you
So very tenderly
I tell of your beauty
How it lives inside of me
I tell you of my longing
To hold you again
To feel our hearts beat as one
As we did way back then
To see your smiling eyes
As I adore your beautiful face
You are sweet sixteen, it's 61
No aging taken place
Each night I write love letters
Instead of counting sheep
To say how much I love you
Before I go to sleep

ANGEL WINGS

He pulls out her photo
From time to time
So securely hidden
So sweet to find
The rivers of time
Could never erase
The emerald from the eyes
Within her perfect face
Transfixed on her image
In the still of the night
He sees angel wings
A halo of white light
He feels her love so sweetly
It is the purest kind
As she wraps him in angel wings
As he holds her in his mind

YOU BLESS MY DAY

His heart
Was such a lonely place?
Was so cold, barren and rocky
Unkempt with disgrace
Was so wonderful then
You came into sight
Lifted him as the falcon
How elegant the flight
Inside his heart
Once stone, ice and snow
Is filled with warmth
Where flowers of beauty grow
Forever to remember
Forever to bless the day
When you brought happiness
And blessed his way

SEASONS

A bit of chill
In the November wind
But like the blown leaf of autumn
You're in my mind again
As the feel of spiced wine
Coursing through my veins
I feel the warmth of your love
As it flows in my heart again
Into the deep of winter
I feel you inside my soul
Giving warmth and comfort
As the glowing embers of burning coal
It is in the springtime
All things to renew
A season of growing
Oh, how I love you
It is into the mid of July
The heat is so much higher
My love for you, is once again
A raging roaring wildfire?

BONDING OF THE SOUL

It is his mission
Which two hearts need
One which
Shall surely succeed
To melt the two
With the fires of love's glow
Bond each together
At the other's soul
What happiness
Will surely be
As he is now half of her
And she is now half of he

YOU ARE THAT

You are that
Which God has wrought?
You fill my mind
With constant thought
And as your beauty I behold
You fill the reaches
Of my soul
You are a waltz
You are a song
I have searched for you
Oh so long
Though you say
We never be
I shall love you
Throughout eternity

FOR THE SOUND OF YOUR VOICE

I could spend a lifetime
Had I the choice
Listening to the melody
Of your lovely voice
It is so so sweet
With perfect harmony
How it resonated
Deep into the soul of me
Or were it to be
In my powers
I could listen to you saying nothing
For hours after hours
So it would seem
I have little choice
I shall spend my lifetime listening
For the sound of your lovely voice

A CASE OF MISSING YOU

I have a terminal case
Of the I'm missing you
Pains like a tooth
Aches like the flu
Aching deep inside
All the way to the bone
Seems my arms and legs
Are completely gone
My head once full
Of grey matter
Now is only
Clank and clatter
Dare I tell you?
About my heart
Feels completely
Torn apart
Only remedy
I can see
Please come home
Doctor me.

COTTAGE BY THE SEA

Patiently he sat there
In his cottage by the sea
He felt sad and so alone
But now he was free
There came a knock upon his door
There flowed such a surprise
An illusion?
She was standing there
He could hardly believe his eyes
He struggled to speak
His voice simply faded away
He ran his fingers through golden locks
Which so long ago had turned to grey
He clung to her gently
Flooding her over with hot tears
Washing away the loneliness and heartaches
And the fading of all the waiting years
Bonded together forever
They shall forever be
Love has brought them together
In the cottage by the sea

THE LAST GOODBYE

He was an old man dying
In the hospital bed
The moments of his lifetime
Were flashing inside his head
But when his mind saw her
He began to smile
Now viewing in slow motion
He would linger a while
Once again he was there
In the familiar place
How he loved her emerald eyes
And the beauty of her face
How sweet the kisses
As they flowed into his heart
Removing all the sorrow
Of the lifetime, being apart.
Once again the feeling
She was his, alone
He said I hear my father calling
It is time, I must go home.

THE JOURNEY

She was sitting in her rocker
Was an old folks home
Her once bright eyes so sad
She was lonely and alone

Her once honey complexion
Was now of winter gray
And the emerald in her eyes
Tears, had slowly washed away

She felt the presence
Of the one she had come to know
Was it only yesterday?
Or was it a lifetime ago?

Could it really be the young lad?
Whom she had come to love
Now an angelic being
Sent from heaven above

This moment in a lifetime
She had forever yearned
She whispered to him quietly
I knew you would return.

Taking her frail, delicate hand

He said just wait and see
Our father has given me the power
To make you an angel like me

Was it so enthroning?
When in the entire night
The two were flashing
With heaven's holy light.

Was in the fiery chariot
Guided by a hundred flashing celestial equine
Set forth they on a heavenly journey
In quest for the end of time.

THE BEGINNING

ACKNOWLEDGMENTS

My heartfelt gratitude to Lauren Eckhardt, Taylor Harvey, and Gail Starck. You have made my dream come true.

To my lovely daughter Melanie Ann Poynor: Thank you for your lifetime of love and support.

Printed in the USA
CPSIA information can be obtained
at www.ICGtesting.com
LVHW040354220124
769411LV00104B/1104